LANDSCAPE and SILENCE

Harold Pinter was born in London in 1930. He is married to Antonia Fraser.

HAROLD PINTER

Landscape
and
Silence

faber and faber

LONDON · BOSTON

First published by Methuen and Co. Ltd in 1969
Paperback edition first published in 1970
First published in this edition in 1991
by Faber and Faber Limited
3 Queen Square London WC1N 3AU

Printed in England by Clays Ltd, St Ives plc

A CIP record for this book is available from the British Library

ISBN 0-571-16087-5

CONTENTS

Landscape

Landscape was first presented on radio by the BBC on 25 April 1968, with the following cast:

BETH	Peggy Ashcroft
DUFF	Eric Porter

Directed by Guy Vaesen

The play was first presented on the stage by the Royal Shakespeare Company at the Aldwych Theatre on 2 July 1969, with the following cast:

BETH	Peggy Ashcroft
DUFF	David Waller

Directed by Peter Hall

A television version of the play appeared on BBC 2 on 4 February 1983 with the following cast:

BETH	Dorothy Tutin
DUFF	Colin Blakely

Directed by Kenneth Ives

DUFF: a man in his early fifties.
BETH: a woman in her late forties.
The kitchen of a country house.
A long kitchen table.
BETH sits in an armchair, which stands away from the table, to its left.
DUFF sits in a chair at the right corner of the table. The background, of a sink, stove, etc., and a window, is dim. Evening.

NOTE:

DUFF *refers normally to* BETH, *but does not appear to hear her voice.*
BETH *never looks at* DUFF, *and does not appear to hear his voice.*
Both characters are relaxed, in no sense rigid.

I would like to stand by the sea. It is there.

Pause

I have. Many times. It's something I cared for. I've done it.

Pause

I'll stand on the beach. On the beach. Well . . . it was very fresh. But it was hot, in the dunes. But it was so fresh, on the shore. I loved it very much.

Pause

Lots of people . . .

Pause

People move so easily. Men. Men move.

Pause

I walked from the dune to the shore. My man slept in the dune. He turned over as I stood. His eyelids. Belly button. Snoozing how lovely.

Pause

Would you like a baby? I said. Children? Babies? Of our own? Would be nice.

Pause

Women turn, look at me.

Pause

Our own child? Would you like that?

Pause

Two women looked at me, turned and stared. No. I was walking, they were still. I turned.

Pause

Why do you look?

Pause

I didn't say that, I stared. Then I was looking at them.

Pause

I am beautiful.

Pause

I walked back over the sand. He had turned. Toes under sand, head buried in his arms.

DUFF

The dog's gone. I didn't tell you.

Pause

I had to shelter under a tree for twenty minutes yesterday. Because of the rain. I meant to tell you. With some youngsters. I didn't know them.

Pause

Then it eased. A downfall. I walked up as far as the pond. Then I felt a couple of big drops. Luckily I was only a few yards from the shelter. I sat down in there. I meant to tell you.

Pause

Do you remember the weather yesterday? That downfall.?

BETH

He felt my shadow. He looked up at me standing above him.

DUFF

I should have had some bread with me. I could have fed the birds.

BETH

Sand on his arms.

DUFF

They were hopping about. Making a racket.

BETH

I lay down by him, not touching.

DUFF

There wasn't anyone else in the shelter. There was a man and woman, under the trees, on the other side of the pond. I didn't feel like getting wet. I stayed where I was.

Pause

Yes, I've forgotten something. The dog was with me.

Pause

BETH

Did those women know me? I didn't remember their faces. I'd never seen their faces before. I'd never seen those women before. I'm certain of it. Why were they looking at me? There's nothing strange about me. There's nothing strange about the way I look. I look like anyone.

DUFF

The dog wouldn't have minded me feeding the birds. Anyway, as soon as we got in the shelter he fell asleep. But even if he'd been awake . . . . .

Pause

BETH

They all held my arm lightly, as I stepped out of the car, or out of the door, or down the steps. Without exception. If they touched the back of my neck, or my hand, it was done so lightly. Without exception. With one exception.

DUFF

Mind you, there was a lot of shit all over the place, all along the paths, by the pond. Dogshit, duckshit . . . all kinds of shit . . . all over the paths. The rain didn't clean it up. It made it even more treacherous.

Pause

The ducks were well away, right over on their island. But I wouldn't have fed them, anyway. I would have fed the sparrows.

BETH

I could stand now. I could be the same. I dress differently, but I am beautiful.

Silence

DUFF

You should have a walk with me one day down to the pond, bring some bread. There's nothing to stop you.

Pause

I sometimes run into one or two people I know. You might remember them.

Pause

BETH

When I watered the flowers he stood, watching me, and watched me arrange them. My gravity, he said. I was so grave, attending

to the flowers, I'm going to water and arrange the flowers, I
said. He followed me and watched, standing at a distance from
me. When the arrangement was done I stayed still. I heard
him moving. He didn't touch me. I listened. I looked at the
flowers, blue and white, in the bowl.

Pause

Then he touched me.

Pause

He touched the back of my neck. His fingers, lightly, touching,
lightly, touching, the back, of my neck.

DUFF

The funny thing was, when I looked, when the shower was
over, the man and woman under the trees on the other side of
the pond had gone. There wasn't a soul in the park.

BETH

I wore a white beach robe. Underneath I was naked.

Pause

There wasn't a soul on the beach. Very far away a man was
sitting, on a breakwater. But even so he was only a pinpoint,
in the sun. And even so I could only see him when I was
standing, or on my way from the shore to the dune. When I
lay down I could no longer see him, therefore he couldn't see
me.

Pause

I may have been mistaken. Perhaps the beach was empty.
Perhaps there was no-one there.

Pause

He couldn't see .. my man .. anyway. He never stood up.

Pause

Snoozing how lovely I said to him. But I wasn't a fool, on that occasion. I lay quiet, by his side.

Silence

DUFF

Anyway . . .

BETH

My skin . . .

DUFF

I'm sleeping all right these days.

BETH

Was stinging.

DUFF

Right through the night, every night.

BETH

I'd been in the sea.

DUFF

Maybe it's something to do with the fishing. Getting to learn more about fish.

BETH

Stinging in the sea by myself.

DUFF

They're very shy creatures. You've got to woo them. You must never get excited with them. Or flurried. Never.

BETH

I knew there must be a hotel near, where we could get some tea.

Silence

DUFF

Anyway . . . luck was on my side for a change. By the time I got out of the park the pubs were open.

Pause

So I thought I might as well pop in and have a pint. I wanted to tell you. I met some nut in there. First of all I had a word with the landlord. He knows me. Then this nut came in. He ordered a pint and he made a criticism of the beer. I had no patience with it.

BETH

But then I thought perhaps the hotel bar will be open. We'll sit in the bar. He'll buy me a drink. What will I order? But what will he order? What will he want? I shall hear him say it. I shall hear his voice. He will ask me what I would like first. Then he'll order the two drinks. I shall hear him do it.

DUFF

This beer is piss, he said. Undrinkable. There's nothing wrong with the beer, I said. Yes there is, he said, I just told you what was wrong with it. It's the best beer in the area, I said. No it isn't, this chap said, it's piss. The landlord picked up the mug and had a sip. Good beer, he said. Someone's made a mistake, this fellow said, someone's used this pintpot instead of the boghole.

Pause

The landlord threw a half a crown on the bar and told him to take it. The pint's only two and three, the man said, I owe you three pence, but I haven't got any change. Give the threepence to your son, the landlord said, with my compliments. I haven't got a son, the man said, I've never had any children. I bet you're not even married, the landlord said. This man said: I'm not married. No-one'll marry me.

Pause

Then the man asked the landlord and me if we would have a drink with him. The landlord said he'd have a pint. I didn't answer at first, but the man came over to me and said: Have one with *me*. Have one with *me*.

Pause

He put down a ten bob note and said he'd have a pint as well.

Silence

BETH

Suddenly I stood. I walked to the shore and into the water. I didn't swim. I don't swim. I let the water billow me. I rested in the water. The waves were very light, delicate. They touched the back of my neck.

Silence

DUFF

One day when the weather's good you could go out into the garden and sit down. You'd like that. The open air. I'm often out there. The dog liked it.

Pause

I've put in some flowers. You'd find it pleasant. Looking at the flowers. You could cut a few if you liked. Bring them in. No-one would see you. There's no-one there.

Pause

That's where we're lucky, in my opinion. To live in Mr Sykes' house in peace, no-one to bother us. I've thought of inviting one or two people I know from the village in here for a bit of a drink once or twice but I decided against it. It's not necessary.

Pause

You know what you get quite a lot of out in the garden? Butterflies.

BETH

I slipped out of my costume and put on my beachrobe. Underneath I was naked. There wasn't a soul on the beach. Except for an elderly man, far away on a breakwater. I lay down beside him and whispered. Would you like a baby? A child? Of our own? Would be nice.

Pause

DUFF

What did you think of that downfall?

Pause

Of course the youngsters I met under the first tree, during the first shower, they were larking about and laughing. I tried to listen, to find out what they were laughing about, but I couldn't work it out. They were whispering. I tried to listen, to find out what the joke was.

Pause

Anyway I didn't find out.

Pause

I was thinking ... when you were young ... you didn't laugh much. You were ... grave.

Silence

BETH

That's why he'd picked such a desolate place. So that I could draw in peace. I had my sketch book with me. I took it out. I took my drawing pencil out. But there was nothing to draw. Only the beach, the sea.

Pause

Could have drawn him. He didn't want it. He laughed.

Pause

I laughed, with him.

Pause

I waited for him to laugh, then I would smile, turn away, he would touch my back, turn me, to him. My nose .. creased. I would laugh with him, a little.

Pause

He laughed. I'm sure of it. So I didn't draw him.

Silence

DUFF

You were a first-rate housekeeper when you were young. Weren't you? I was very proud. You never made a fuss, you never got into a state, you went about your work. He could rely on you. He did. He trusted you, to run his house, to keep the house up to the mark, no panic.

Pause

Do you remember when I took him on that trip to the north? That long trip. When we got back he thanked you for looking after the place so well, everything running like clockwork.

Pause

You'd missed me. When I came into this room you stopped still. I had to walk all the way over the floor towards you.

Pause

I touched you.

Pause

But I had something to say to you, didn't I? I waited, I didn't say it then, but I'd made up my mind to say it, I'd decided I would say it, and I did say it, the next morning. Didn't I?

Pause

I told you that I'd let you down. I'd been unfaithful to you.

Pause

You didn't cry. We had a few hours off. We walked up to the pond, with the dog. We stood under the trees for a bit. I didn't know why you'd brought that carrier bag with you. I asked you. I said what's in that bag? It turned out to be bread. You fed the ducks. Then we stood under the trees and looked across the pond.

Pause

When we got back into this room you put your hands on my face and you kissed me.

BETH

But I didn't really want a drink.

Pause

I drew a face in the sand, then a body. The body of a woman.
Then the body of a man, close to her, not touching. But they
didn't look like anything. They didn't look like human figures.
The sand kept on slipping, mixing the contours. I crept close
to him and put my head on his arm, and closed my eyes. All
those darting red and black flecks, under my eyelid. I moved my
cheek on his skin. And all those darting red and black flecks,
moving about under my eyelid. I buried my face in his side
and shut the light out.

Silence

DUFF

Mr Sykes took to us from the very first interview, didn't he?

Pause

He said I've got the feeling you'll make a very good team. Do
you remember? And that's what we proved to be. No question.
I could drive well, I could polish his shoes well, I earned my
keep. Turn my hand to anything. He never lacked for anything, in the way of being looked after. Mind you, he was a
gloomy bugger.

Pause

I was never sorry for him, at any time, for his lonely life.

Pause

That nice blue dress he chose for you, for the house, that was
very nice of him. Of course it was in his own interests for you
to look good about the house, for guests.

BETH

He moved in the sand and put his arm around me.

Silence

DUFF

Do you like me to talk to you?

Pause

Do you like me to tell you about all the things I've been doing?

Pause

About all the things I've been thinking?

Pause

Mmmnn?

Pause

I think you do.

BETH

And cuddled me.

Silence

DUFF

Of course it was in his own interests to see that you were attractively dressed about the house, to give a good impression to his guests.

BETH

I caught a bus to the crossroads and then walked down the lane by the old church. It was very quiet, except for birds. There was an old man fiddling about on the cricket pitch, bending. I stood out of the sun, under a tree.

Pause

I heard the car. He saw me and stopped me. I stayed still. Then the car moved again, came towards me slowly. I moved round the front of it, in the dust. I couldn't see him for the sun, but he was watching me. When I got to the door it was locked. I looked through at him. He leaned over and opened the door. I got in and sat beside him. He smiled at me. Then he reversed, all in one movement, very quickly, quite straight, up the lane to the crossroads, and we drove to the sea.

Pause

DUFF

We're the envy of a lot of people, you know, living in this house, having this house all to ourselves. It's too big for two people.

BETH

He said he knew a very desolate beach, that no-one else in the world knew, and that's where we are going.

DUFF

I was very gentle to you. I was kind to you, that day. I knew you'd had a shock, so I was gentle with you. I held your arm on the way back from the pond. You put your hands on my face and kissed me.

BETH

All the food I had in my bag I had cooked myself, or prepared myself. I had baked the bread myself.

DUFF

The girl herself I considered unimportant. I didn't think it necessary to go into details. I decided against it.

BETH

The windows were open but we kept the hood up.

Pause

DUFF

Mr Sykes gave a little dinner party that Friday. He complimented you on your cooking and the service.

Pause

Two women. That was all. Never seen them before. Probably his mother and sister.

Pause

They wanted coffee late. I was in bed. I fell asleep. I would have come down to the kitchen to give you a hand but I was too tired.

Pause

But I woke up when you got into bed. You were out on your feet. You were asleep as soon as you hit the pillow. Your body . . . just fell back.

BETH

He was right. It was desolate. There wasn't a soul on the beach.

Silence

DUFF

I had a look over the house the other day. I meant to tell you. The dust is bad. We'll have to polish it up.

Pause

We could go up to the drawing room, open the windows. I could wash the old decanters. We could have a drink up there one evening, if it's a pleasant evening.

Pause

I think there's moths. I moved the curtain and they flew out.

Pause

BETH

Of course when I'm older I won't be the same as I am, I won't be what I am, my skirts, my long legs, I'll be older, I won't be the same.

DUFF

At least now ... at least now, I can walk down to the pub in peace and up to the pond in peace, with no-one to nag the shit out of me.

Silence

BETH

All it is, you see ... I said ... is the lightness of your touch, the lightness of your look, my neck, your eyes, the silence, that is my meaning, the loveliness of my flowers, my hands touching my flowers, that is my meaning.

Pause

I've watched other people. I've seen them.

Pause

All the cars zooming by. Men with girls at their sides. Bouncing up and down. They're dolls. They squeak.

Pause

All the people were squeaking in the hotel bar. The girls had long hair. They were smiling.

DUFF

That's what matters, anyway. We're together. That's what matters.

Silence

BETH

But I was up early. There was still plenty to be done and
cleared up. I had put the plates in the sink to soak. They had
soaked overnight. They were easy to wash. The dog was
up. He followed me. Misty morning. Comes from the river.

DUFF

This fellow knew bugger all about beer. He didn't know I'd
been trained as a cellarman. That's why I could speak with
authority.

BETH

I opened the door and went out. There was no-one about.
The sun was shining. Wet, I mean wetness, all over the
ground.

DUFF

A cellarman is the man responsible. He's the earliest up in the
morning. Give the drayman a hand with the barrels. Down
the slide through the cellarflaps. Lower them by rope to the
racks. Rock them on the belly, put a rim up them, use balance
and leverage, hike them up onto the racks.

BETH

Still misty, but thinner, thinning.

DUFF

The bung is on the vertical, in the bunghole. Spile the bung.
Hammer the spile through the centre of the bung. That lets
the air through the bung, down the bunghole, lets the beer
breathe.

BETH

Wetness all over the air. Sunny. Trees like feathers.

DUFF

Then you hammer the tap in.

BETH

I wore my blue dress.

DUFF

Let it stand for three days. Keep wet sacks over the barrels. Hose the cellar floor daily. Hose the barrels daily.

BETH

It was a beautiful autumn morning.

DUFF

Run water through the pipes to the bar pumps daily.

BETH

I stood in the mist.

DUFF

Pull off. Pull off. Stop pulling just before you get to the dregs. The dregs'll give you the shits. You've got an ullage barrel. Feed the slops back to the ullage barrel, send them back to the brewery.

BETH

In the sun.

DUFF

Dip the barrels daily with a brass rod. Know your gallonage. Chalk it up. Then you're tidy. Then you never get caught short.

BETH

Then I went back to the kitchen and sat down.

Pause

DUFF

This chap in the pub said he was surprised to hear it. He said he was surprised to hear about hosing the cellar floor. He said he thought most cellars had a thermostatically controlled cooling system. He said he thought keg beer was fed with oxygen through a cylinder. I said I wasn't talking about keg beer, I was talking about normal draught beer. He said he thought they piped the beer from a tanker into metal containers. I said they may do, but he wasn't talking about the quality of beer I was. He accepted that point.

Pause

BETH

The dog sat down by me. I stroked him. Through the window I could see down into the valley. I saw children in the valley. They were running through the grass. They ran up the hill.

Long Silence

DUFF

I never saw your face. You were standing by the windows. One of those black nights. A downfall. All I could hear was the rain on the glass, smacking on the glass. You knew I'd come in but you didn't move. I stood close to you. What were you looking at? It was black outside. I could just see your shape in the window, your reflection. There must have been some kind of light somewhere. Perhaps just your face reflected, lighter than all the rest. I stood close to you. Perhaps you were just thinking, in a dream. Without touching you, I could feel your bottom.

Silence

BETH

I remembered always, in drawing, the basic principles of

shadow and light. Objects intercepting the light cast shadows. Shadow is deprivation of light. The shape of the shadow is determined by that of the object. But not always. Not always directly. Sometimes it is only indirectly affected by it. Sometimes the cause of the shadow cannot be found.

Pause

But I always bore in mind the basic principles of drawing.

Pause

So that I never lost track. Or heart.

Pause

DUFF

You used to wear a chain round your waist. On the chain you carried your keys, your thimble, your notebook, your pencil, your scissors.

Pause

You stood in the hall and banged the gong.

Pause

What the bloody hell are you doing banging that bloody gong?

Pause

It's bullshit. Standing in an empty hall banging a bloody gong. There's no one to listen. No one'll hear. There's not a soul in the house. Except me. There's nothing for lunch. There's nothing cooked. No stew. No pie. No greens. No joint. Fuck all.

Pause

BETH

So that I never lost track. Even though, even when, I asked

him to turn, to look at me, but he turned to look at me but I couldn't see his look.

Pause

I couldn't see whether he was looking at me.

Pause

Although he had turned. And appeared to be looking at me.

DUFF

I took the chain off and the thimble, the keys, the scissors slid off it and clattered down. I booted the gong down the hall. The dog came in. I thought you would come to me, I thought you would come into my arms and kiss me, even ... offer yourself to me. I would have had you in front of the dog, like a man, in the hall, on the stone, banging the gong, mind you don't get the scissors up your arse, or the thimble, don't worry, I'll throw them for the dog to chase, the thimble will keep the dog happy, he'll play with it with his paws, you'll plead with me like a woman, I'll bang the gong on the floor, if the sound is too flat, lacks resonance, I'll hang it back on its hook, bang you against it swinging, gonging, waking the place up, calling them all for dinner, lunch is up, bring out the bacon, bang your lovely head, mind the dog doesn't swallow the thimble, slam—

Silence

BETH

He lay above me and looked down at me. He supported my shoulder.

Pause

So tender his touch on my neck. So softly his kiss on my cheek.

Pause

My hand on his rib.

Pause

So sweetly the sand over me. Tiny the sand on my skin.

Pause

So silent the sky in my eyes. Gently the sound of the tide.

Pause

Oh my true love I said.

Silence

Silence was first presented by the Royal Shakespeare Company at the Aldwych Theatre on 2nd July, 1969, with the following cast:

ELLEN: a girl in her twenties	Frances Cuka
RUMSEY: a man of forty	Anthony Bate
BATES: a man in his middle thirties	Norman Rodway

Directed by Peter Hall

Three areas.
A chair in each area.

RUMSEY

I walk with my girl who wears a grey blouse when she walks
and grey shoes and walks with me readily wearing her clothes
considered for me. Her grey clothes.

She holds my arm.

On good evenings we walk through the hills to the top of the
hill past the dogs the clouds racing just before dark or as dark
is falling when the moon

When it's chilly I stop her and slip her raincoat over her
shoulders or rainy slip arms into the arms, she twisting her
arms. And talk to her and tell her everything.

She dresses for my eyes.

I tell her my thoughts. Now I am ready to walk, her arm in
me her hand in me.

I tell her my life's thoughts, clouds racing. She looks up at
me or listens looking down. She stops in midsentence, my
sentence, to look up at me. Sometimes her hand has slipped
from mine, her arm loosened, she walks slightly apart, dog
barks.

ELLEN

There are two. One who is with me sometimes, and another.
He listens to me. I tell him what I know. We walk by the dogs.

Sometimes the wind is so high he does not hear me. I lead him to a tree, clasp closely to him and whisper to him, wind going, dogs stop, and he hears me.

But the other hears me.

BATES

Caught a bus to the town. Crowds. Lights round the market, rain and stinking. Showed her the bumping lights. Took her down around the dumps. Black roads and girders. She clutching me. This way the way I bring you. Pubs throw the doors smack into the night. Cars barking and the lights. She with me, clutching.

Brought her into this place, my cousin runs it. Undressed her, placed my hand.

ELLEN

I go by myself with the milk to the top, the clouds racing, all the blue changes, I'm dizzy sometimes, meet with him under some place.

One time visited his house. He put a light on, it reflected the window, it reflected in the window.

RUMSEY

She walks from the door to the window to see the way she has come, to confirm that the house which grew nearer is the same one she stands in, that the path and the bushes are the same, that the gate is the same. When I stand beside her and smile at her, she looks at me and smiles.

BATES

How many times standing clenched in the pissing dark waiting ?

The mud, the cows, the river.

You cross the field out of darkness. You arrive.

You stand breathing before me. You smile.

I put my hands on your shoulders and press. Press the smile off your face.

ELLEN

There are two. I turn to them and speak. I look them in their eyes. I kiss them there and say, I look away to smile, and touch them as I turn.

Silence

RUMSEY

I watch the clouds. Pleasant the ribs and tendons of cloud.

I've lost nothing.

Pleasant alone and watch the folding light. My animals are quiet. My heart never bangs. I read in the evenings. There is no-one to tell me what is expected or not expected of me. There is nothing required of me.

BATES

I'm at my last gasp with this unendurable racket. I kicked open the door and stood before them. Someone called me Grandad and told me to button it. It's they should button it. Were I young . . .

One of them told me I was lucky to be alive, that I would have to bear it in order to pay for being alive, in order to give thanks for being alive.

It's a question of sleep. I need something of it, or how can I remain alive, without any true rest, having no solace, no constant solace, not even any damn inconstant solace.

I am strong, but not as strong as the bastards in the other room, and their tittering bitches, and their music, and their love.

If I changed my life, perhaps, and lived deliberately at night, and slept in the day. But what exactly would I do? What can be meant by living in the dark?

ELLEN

Now and again I meet my drinking companion and have a drink with her. She is a friendly woman, quite elderly, quite friendly. But she knows little of me, she could never know much of me, not really, not now. She's funny. She starts talking sexily to me, in the corner, with our drinks. I laugh.

She asks me about my early life, when I was young, never departing from her chosen subject, but I have nothing to tell her about the sexual part of my youth. I'm old, I tell her, my youth was somewhere else, anyway I don't remember. She does the talking anyway.

I like to get back to my room. It has a pleasant view. I have one or two friends, ladies. They ask me where I come from. I say of course from the country. I don't see much of them.

I sometimes wonder if I think. I heard somewhere about how many thoughts go through the brain of a person. But I couldn't remember anything I'd actually thought, for some time.

It isn't something that anyone could ever tell me, could ever reassure me about, nobody could tell, from looking at me, what was happening.

But I'm still quite pretty really, quite nice eyes, nice skin.

BATES *moves to* ELLEN

BATES

Will we meet to-night?

ELLEN

I don't know.

Pause

BATES

Come with me to-night.

ELLEN

Where?

BATES

Anywhere. For a walk.

Pause

ELLEN

I don't want to walk.

BATES

Why not?

Pause

ELLEN

I want to go somewhere else.

Pause

                    BATES

Where?

                    ELLEN

I don't know.

Pause

                    BATES

What's wrong with a walk?

                    ELLEN

I don't want to walk.

Pause

                    BATES

What do you want to do?

                    ELLEN

I don't know.

Pause

                    BATES

Do you want to go anywhere else?

                    ELLEN

Yes.

                    BATES

Where?

                    ELLEN

I don't know.

Pause

BATES

Do you want me to buy you a drink?

ELLEN

No.

Pause

BATES

Come for a walk.

ELLEN

No.

Pause

BATES

All right. I'll take you on a bus to the town. I know a place. My cousin runs it.

ELLEN

No.

Silence

RUMSEY

It is curiously hot. Sitting weather, I call it. The weather sits, does not move. Unusual. I shall walk down to my horse and see how my horse is. He'll come towards me.

Perhaps he doesn't need me. My visit, my care, will be like any other visit, any other care. I can't believe it.

BATES

I walk in my mind. But can't get out of the walls, into a wind.

Meadows are walled, and lakes. The sky's a wall.

Once I had a little girl. I took it for walks. I held it by its hand. It looked up at me and said, I see something in a tree, a shape, a shadow. It is leaning down. It is looking at us.

Maybe it's a bird, I said, a big bird, resting. Birds grow tired, after they've flown over the country, up and down in the wind, looking down on all the sights, so sometimes, when they reach a tree, with good solid branches, they rest.

Silence

ELLEN

When I run . . . when I run . . . when I run . . . over the grass . . .

RUMSEY

She floats . . . under me. Floating . . . under me.

ELLEN

I turn. I turn. I wheel. I glide. I wheel. In stunning light. The horizon moves from the sun. I am crushed by the light.

Silence

RUMSEY

Sometimes I see people. They walk towards me, no, not so, walk in my direction, but never reaching me, turning left, or disappearing, and then reappearing, to disappear into the wood.

So many ways to lose sight of them, then to recapture sight of them. They are sharp at first sight . . . then smudged . . . then lost . . . then glimpsed again . . . then gone.

BATES

Funny. Sometimes I press my hand on my forehead, calmingly, feel all the dust drain out, let it go, feel the grit slip away. Funny moment. That calm moment.

ELLEN *moves to* RUMSEY

ELLEN

It's changed. You've painted it. You've made shelves. Everything. It's beautiful.

RUMSEY

Can you remember . . . when you were here last?

ELLEN

Oh yes.

RUMSEY

You were a little girl.

ELLEN

I was.

Pause

RUMSEY

Can you cook now?

ELLEN

Shall I cook for you?

RUMSEY

Yes.

ELLEN

Next time I come. I will.

Pause

RUMSEY

Do you like music?

ELLEN

Yes.

RUMSEY

I'll play you music.
Pause

RUMSEY

Look at your reflection.

ELLEN

Where?

RUMSEY

In the window.

ELLEN

It's very dark outside.

RUMSEY

It's high up.

ELLEN

Does it get darker the higher you get?

RUMSEY

No.
Silence

ELLEN

Around me sits the night. Such a silence. I can hear myself. Cup my ear. My heart beats in my ear. Such a silence. Is it me? Am I silent or speaking? How can I know? Can I know such things? No-one has ever told me. I need to be told things. I seem to be old. Am I old now? No-one will tell me. I must find a person to tell me these things.

BATES

My landlady asks me in for a drink. Stupid conversation. What are you doing here? Why do you live alone? Where do you come from? What do you do with yourself? What kind of life have you had? You seem fit. A bit grumpy. You can smile, surely, at something? Surely you have smiled, at a thing in your life? At something? Has there been no pleasant-ness in your life? No kind of loveliness in your life? Are you nothing but a childish old man, suffocating himself?

I've had all that. I've got all that. I said.

ELLEN

He sat me on his knee, by the window, and asked if he could kiss my right cheek. I nodded he could. He did. Then he asked, if, having kissed my right, he could do the same with my left. I said yes. He did.

Silence

RUMSEY

She was looking down. I couldn't hear what she said.

BATES

I can't hear you. Yes you can, I said.

RUMSEY

What are you saying? Look at me, she said.

BATES
I didn't. I didn't hear you, she said. I didn't hear what you said.

RUMSEY
But I am looking at you. It's your head that's bent.

Silence

BATES
The little girl looked up at me. I said: at night horses are quite happy. They stand about, then after a bit of a time they go to sleep. In the morning they wake up, snort a bit, canter, sometimes, and eat. You've no cause to worry about them.

ELLEN *moves to* RUMSEY

RUMSEY
Find a young man.

ELLEN
There aren't any.

RUMSEY
Don't be stupid.

ELLEN
I don't like them.

RUMSEY
You're stupid.

ELLEN

I hate them.

Pause

RUMSEY

Find one.

Silence

BATES

For instance, I said, those shapes in the trees, you'll find they're just birds, resting after a long journey.

ELLEN

I go up with the milk. The sky hits me. I walk in this wind to collide with them waiting.

There are two. They halt to laugh and bellow in the yard. They dig and punch and cackle where they stand. They turn to move, look round at me to grin. I turn my eyes from one, and from the other to him.

Silence

BATES

From the young people's room – silence. Sleep? Tender love?

It's of no importance.

Silence

RUMSEY

I walk with my girl who wears—

BATES

Caught a bus to the town. Crowds. Lights round—

Silence

ELLEN

After my work each day I walk back through people but I don't notice them. I'm not in a dream or anything of that sort. On the contrary. I'm quite wide awake to the world around me. But not to the people. There must be something in them to notice, to pay attention to, something of interest in them. In fact I know there is. I'm certain of it. But I pass through them noticing nothing. It is only later, in my room, that I remember. Yes, I remember. But I'm never sure that what I remember is of to-day or of yesterday or of a long time ago.

And then often it is only half things I remember, half things, beginnings of things.

My drinking companion for the hundredth time asked me if I'd ever been married. This time I told her I had. Yes, I told her I had. Certainly. I can remember the wedding.

Silence

RUMSEY

On good evenings we walk through the hills to the top of the hill past the dogs the clouds racing

ELLEN

Sometimes the wind is so high he does not hear me.

BATES

Brought her into this place, my cousin runs it.

ELLEN

all the blue changes, I'm dizzy sometimes

Silence

RUMSEY

that the path and the bushes are the same, that the gate is the same

BATES

You cross the field out of darkness.
You arrive.

ELLEN

I turn to them and speak.

Silence

RUMSEY

and watch the folding light.

BATES

and their tittering bitches, and their music, and their love.

ELLEN

They ask me where I come from. I say of course from the country.

Silence

                          BATES
Come with me tonight.

                          ELLEN
Where?

                          BATES
Anywhere. For a walk.

Silence

                          RUMSEY
My visit, my care, will be like any other visit, any other care.

                          BATES
I see something in a tree, a shape, a shadow.

Silence

                          ELLEN
When I run . . .

                          RUMSEY
Floating . . . under me.

                          ELLEN
The horizon moves from the sun.

Silence

                          RUMSEY
They are sharp at first sight . . . then smudged . . . then lost . . .
then glimpsed again . . . then gone.

                          BATES
feel all the dust drain out, let it go,

feel the grit slip away.

ELLEN

I look them in their eyes.

Silence

RUMSEY

It's high up.

ELLEN

Does it get darker the higher you get?

RUMSEY

No.

Silence

ELLEN

Around me sits the night. Such a silence.

BATES

I've had all that. I've got all that. I said.

ELLEN

I nodded he could.

Silence

RUMSEY

She was looking down.

BATES

Yes you can, I said.

RUMSEY

What are you saying?

BATES

I didn't hear you, she said.

RUMSEY

But I am looking at you. It's your head that's bent.

Silence

BATES

In the morning they wake up, snort a bit, canter, sometimes, and eat.

Silence

ELLEN

There aren't any.

RUMSEY

Don't be stupid.

ELLEN

I don't like them.

RUMSEY

You're stupid.

Silence

BATES

For instance, I said, those shapes in the trees.

ELLEN

I walk in this wind to collide with them waiting.

Silence

BATES

Sleep? Tender love? It's of no importance.

ELLEN

I kiss them there and say

Silence

RUMSEY

I walk

Silence

BATES

Caught a bus

Silence

ELLEN

Certainly. I can remember the wedding.

Silence

RUMSEY

I walk with my girl who wears a grey blouse

BATES

Caught a bus to the town. Crowds. Lights round the market

Long silence

Fade lights

Night

Night was first presented by Alexander H. Cohen Ltd. in an entertainment entitled *Mixed Doubles* at the Comedy Theatre on 9th April, 1969, with the following cast:

MAN   Nigel Stock
WOMAN   Vivien Merchant
                Directed by Alexander Doré

A woman and a man in their forties.
They sit with coffee.

MAN

I'm talking about that time by the river.

WOMAN

What time?

MAN

The first time. On the bridge. Starting on the bridge.

Pause

WOMAN

I can't remember.

MAN

On the bridge. We stopped and looked down at the river. It was night. There were lamps lit on the towpath. We were alone. We looked up the river. I put my hand on the small of your waist. Don't you remember? I put my hand under your coat.

Pause

WOMAN

Was it winter?

MAN

Of course it was winter. It was when we met. It was our first walk. You must remember that.

WOMAN

I remember walking. I remember walking with you.

MAN

The first time? Our first walk?

WOMAN

Yes, of course I remember that.

Pause

We walked down a road into a field, through some railings. We walked to a corner of the field and then we stood by the railings.

MAN

No. It was on the bridge that we stopped.

Pause

WOMAN

That was someone else.

MAN

Rubbish.

WOMAN

That was another girl.

MAN

It was years ago. You've forgotten.

Pause

I remember the light on the water.

WOMAN

You took my face in your hands, standing by the railings. You were very gentle, you were very caring. You cared. Your eyes searched my face. I wondered who you were. I wondered what you thought. I wondered what you would do.

MAN

You agree we met at a party. You agree with that?

WOMAN

What was that?

MAN

What?

WOMAN

I thought I heard a child crying.

MAN

There was no sound.

WOMAN

I thought it was a child, crying, waking up.

MAN

The house is silent.

Pause

It's very late. We're sitting here. We should be in bed. I have to be up early. I have things to do. Why do you argue?

WOMAN

I don't. I'm not. I'm willing to go to bed. I have things to do. I have to be up in the morning.

Pause

MAN

A man called Doughty gave the party. You knew him. I had met him. I knew his wife. I met you there. You were standing by the window. I smiled at you, and to my surprise you smiled back. You liked me. I was amazed. You found me attractive. Later you told me. You liked my eyes.

WOMAN

You liked mine.

Pause

WOMAN

You touched my hand. You asked me who I was, and what I
was, and whether I was aware that you were touching my
hand, that your fingers were touching mine, that your fingers
were moving up and down between mine.

MAN

No. We stopped on a bridge. I stood behind you. I put my
hand under your coat, onto your waist. You felt my hand on
you.

Pause

WOMAN

We had been to a party. Given by the Doughtys. You had
known his wife. She looked at you dearly, as if to say you
were her dear. She seemed to love you. I didn't. I didn't know
you. They had a lovely house. By a river. I went to collect
my coat, leaving you waiting for me. You had offered to escort
me. I thought you were quite courtly, quite courteous,
pleasantly mannered, quite caring. I slipped my coat on and
looked out of the window, knowing you were waiting. I looked
down over the garden to the river, and saw the lamplight on the
water. Then I joined you and we walked down the road
through railings into a field, must have been some kind of
park. Later we found your car. You drove me.

Pause

MAN

I touched your breasts.

WOMAN

Where?

MAN

On the bridge. I felt your breasts.

WOMAN

Really?

MAN

Standing behind you.

WOMAN

I wondered whether you would, whether you wanted to, whether you would.

MAN

Yes.

WOMAN

I wondered how you would go about it, whether you wanted to, sufficiently.

MAN

I put my hands under your sweater, I undid your brassière, I felt your breasts.

WOMAN

Another night perhaps. Another girl.

MAN

You don't remember my fingers on your skin?

WOMAN

Were they in your hands? My breasts? Fully in your hands?

MAN

You don't remember my hands on your skin?

Pause

WOMAN

Standing behind me?

MAN

Yes.

WOMAN

But my back was against railings. I felt the railings . . behind me. You were facing me. I was looking into your eyes. My coat was closed. It was cold.

MAN

I undid your coat.

WOMAN

It was very late. Chilly.

MAN

And then we left the bridge and we walked down the towpath and we came to a rubbish dump.

WOMAN

And you had me and you told me you had fallen in love with me, and you said you would take care of me always, and you told me my voice and my eyes, my thighs, my breasts, were incomparable, and that you would adore me always.

MAN

Yes I did.

WOMAN

And you do adore me always.

MAN

Yes I do.

WOMAN

And then we had children and we sat and talked and you remembered women on bridges and towpaths and rubbish dumps.

MAN

And you remembered your bottom against railings and men holding your hands and men looking into your eyes.

WOMAN

And talking to me softly.

MAN

And your soft voice. Talking to them softly at night.

WOMAN

And they said I will adore you always.

MAN

Saying I will adore you always.